PRAISE FOR
FOR THE R...

G000141474

This book gives personalised support to young people searching for ways of succeeding in today's hectic world. We have been waiting for such support for a very long time... now it is here! Cel has opened up avenues for success for young adults in a compelling way.

> — **Professor Gloria Agyemang**, *Professor of Accounting, Executive Dean of School of Business and Management at Royal Holloway University of London*

Chapter 7 is my favourite. It inspires me every single time without fail. Seeing how Cel unravels all her experiences makes me appreciate my little achievements even more.

> — **Khadija Mussa**, *BSc Management with Accounting Student at Royal Holloway University of London*

Cel has captured moments which are so relatable to people all over the UK. It's a thoroughly enjoyable read.

> — **Polly Dhaliwal**, *Head of Product at Enterprise Nation and Founder of Girls in Movement Podcast*

Cel shares concise and encouraging advice on how to prepare yourself for success. Her book takes you through a journey of self-discovery, allowing you to be your best self and uncover your full potential. Her words are inspiring, instructive, and insightful. Great read!

— **Garri Davis**, *Entrepreneur and Best-Selling Author*

This book is like having an honest conversation with a trusted friend, philosopher and guide. It takes you on an eye-opening and transformative journey towards the fulfilment of your aspirations. Cel holds an honest and insightful mirror that reveals your inner strengths and areas of improvement and then takes you gently yet firmly by the hand leading you towards your desired destination whilst unveiling a better version of yourself.

— **Professor Sukanya Sen Gupta**, *Professor of Management at Royal Holloway University, University of London Director of MSc Human Resource Management*

Cel takes you on a journey of self-discovery and inspires you to live your truth and love your brilliance!

— **Marianne Cadet**, *Attorney, Public Defender*

This book provides a practical approach to achieve any goal. Definitely a must read!

— *Jackie Harden*, *Best-Selling Author, Life Coach and Speaker*

This is a lucid and candid book that Millennials and Gen Z's in particular will love. It encapsulates Cel's wisdom gleaned from her early career as an entrepreneur trying to find her place in the world. Using copious, relatable examples from her own life, "Prepping for the Real World" is a concise and very readable, reflective, and empowering reader that is loaded up with actionable takeaways.

— *Professor Justin O'Brien*, *National Teaching Fellow, Executive Director for Postgraduate Programmes at the University of Surrey*

Cel's talent of storytelling gives you the gentle but firm push to start designing your life and own career. There are 14 key questions that will allow you to gain a deeper understanding of your own self and thus take charge of your world.

— *Konstantina Dee*, *Careers & Employability Officer at WMG, University of Warwick*

Cel has touched the core of what so many of us experience as we attempt to live the life expected of us. Thank you so much for this reminder of how strong we are at our core. Thank you for reminding us that the innermost and truest version of ourselves is what is required to live out our highest potential. This book is the formula to create your dream life. Can we make this book a required reading for our youth? I surely wish I had this book on my journey to self-discovery.

— **Michelle Johnson**, *MHS, PA-C, The Pain Free PA, Certified Life Coach & Stress Specialist*

With this book, Cel is making her formula for successfully designing your own world more widely available than to the countless organisations and individuals that she has worked with. It is an easy read that nevertheless asks challenging questions to find out where the gaps are between where I am now and where I want to be. Peppered with her own personal experience, this book is a great starting point for anyone who wants to take the next step but isn't sure how to go about being more true to yourself, whether you want to become an entrepreneur, a leader in your field or step up in your organisation.

— **Dr. Sigrun Wagner**, *Head of Department and Senior Lecturer, School of Business and Management, Royal Holloway, University of London*

It is often said that when you're looking to contribute to the world, you should contribute something that you would have found useful before you knew what you now know. This is exactly what Cel has done. She has used her personal experience to create a masterpiece which will help, not just students and young people but anyone who wants to better take control of the circumstances of their life and create a future they desire. Cel openly describes her personal experience, displaying her strength, authenticity and vulnerability as she shares her Formula. A formula that I wish I'd been aware of when I was going through my journey of designing my own world. This Formula is a game changer! It is the secret to a life of being fully, totally and awesomely YOU.

— **Ene Obi**, *Founder of Ziano Mind Spa and Best-Selling Author of Your Life is Calling*

Cel's transparency in the book is a breath of fresh air. This book will give the readers a proved Formula that will bring results in their lives. It will ignite you and place you on the path of moving forward in your life. This is a must read!

— **Esther V. Graham**, *Founder and CEO of Festa Della Donna LLC, Neuro-Transformational Coach*

This book is a true treasure and great guide to help young adults prepare for shifting into adulthood. By following Cel's journey you learn how to get clear on your purpose. Cel's formula works and will guide you and many others to feel more confident in yourself as you create your own business or gain employment for a corporation.

— *Joy LaBelle Clark*, *International Mindfulness Personal Development Coach (IMTA), Fortune 500 Senior Corporate Leader with over 20 years of experience.*

PREPPING FOR
THE REAL WORLD

PREPPING FOR
THE REAL WORLD

STUDENT AND GRADUATE SUCCESS SECRETS

Cel Amade

First published in the UK by Cel Amade 2022

A catalogue record for this book is available from the British Library

ISBN 978–1–3999–0956–3

CONTENTS

INTRODUCTION

I've always wondered how some people could be so gifted and talented at such a young age. As a child, I watched young athletes, actors, singers, performers and dancers in awe — silently thinking how lucky they were to be great at something at such a young age. For years, I didn't know what I was great at, and I didn't know what my gift was. To be quite frank, I didn't even think I had a talent. I thought talents were God-given gifts for the selected few — that some people are born talented, and others are born normal.

Since I believed I had no unique talents, I convinced myself that I had to learn new skills and be good at everything. In school, I lived by the ethic to study hard, get top grades and be the best in all subjects. Because I had no talents to share with the world, being the best student was at the top of my agenda! That strategy worked well for a few years... During my school years, parents looked up to me like the perfect child they never had — wishing deep down inside that their child was as dedicated to learning and studying as I was.

But those parents didn't see that all my efforts to study hard and be good at everything was a loud cry to feel 'gifted'. My dedication to my studies was an attempt to look talented! But unless I was planning to stay in school and study for the rest of my life, without ever stepping into the real world, this strategy couldn't last forever. And sure enough, it didn't last!

I graduated second in a class of three hundred students in a leading UK university, only to realise that I had no clue what I was truly great at. I studied all kinds of books and theories about business management, and I gathered the knowledge, but a piece of the puzzle seemed to be missing when it came to applying that knowledge in the real world. All jobs are respectable if they honour who you truly are. The trouble is, finding that job that honours who you truly are becomes an even more complicated task when you don't know who you truly are in the first place.

Do you know how frustrating it is to look at yourself in the mirror and not recognise your own reflection — to look at your life and know for a fact that this is not how you imagined your twenty-five-year-old self when you were younger — and not know how to shift your life for the better? Have you ever found a job and pretended to enjoy it so that you could feel less like a burden to your friends and family and finally look like a success?

I've done many things to look successful, and I've drained myself and my finances chasing success. I was fixated on the idea of having to learn more, do more and try new things in order to be successful. Each time I tried to be successful, I fell flat on my face! And worst of all, I just couldn't understand why I was not being rewarded for trying. I couldn't understand why life was refusing to reward my new ideas and my learning abilities — because, in school, I was rewarded.

Search and you will find — they say... I searched for success for a long time, and I didn't find it. I searched for new ideas. I tried to improve existing ideas. I searched everywhere! Everywhere, except deep inside my heart and my soul.

This book is the guidance I needed when I was growing up, and it brings me so much joy to share it with you, wherever you are in your life right now... Whether you're just starting university, graduating next year, looking for your first 'real' job, switching careers or trying to find your way — I've written this book with you in mind. If I sound repetitive at times, that's my way of saying pay close attention to this message. Within this book is a formula to help you design your own world. This book is the dose of personal development I wished I had access to ten years ago, and it is my honour that this book has made its way to you.

I celebrate you. I appreciate you. And I encourage you to apply the principles in this book. Thank you for taking a step forward to design your own world! I'm excited for you.

CHAPTER 1

THE JOURNEY BACK TO YOURSELF

If you don't know who you are, how can you design your own world?

▸ When did you first feel like it wasn't okay to be you?

I was eleven years old, and I remember the moment when I felt like it was not okay to be me. You see, I was that skinny kid who didn't wear the latest fashion, travel on every holiday or watch cable TV — yet I was attending a private school with all these well-dressed, multilingual, cool kids. I was the odd, smart little girl who loved to study because my books made me feel understood. When I read my books, I felt powerful and happy. My books never asked me difficult questions — like where my family was planning to go on holiday next term or what I thought about the latest Nickelodeon series. My books knew I could learn something from them, so they were patient enough to teach me what knowledge they contained. My books were happy to summarise all I had just read at the end of every chapter.

On the other hand, my schoolmates assumed I had cable TV at home and that I watched Nickelodeon. When I told them I didn't watch the latest Nickelodeon or Disney series, they had no patience or interest in telling me all about it. Unlike my books, my schoolmates kept the exciting conversations going (without me).

Perhaps that explains why my books felt like better company. As a child, I preferred reading instead of watching cartoons. And every time I earned good grades, I got excited! I got this thrill that filled my heart with joy, and I secretly loved it when teachers read the highest grades aloud. My schoolmates noticed the joy I felt when I earned high grades, and they didn't quite like it. They didn't think that was normal, and because of that, they looked at me differently.

I wasn't the type of girl who boys wanted to hang out with (let alone date), so they avoided me.

The trouble was, the more boys avoided me, the harder I worked to be liked by everyone around me. In order to be friends with the cool girls and accepted by the sporty guys, I concluded that it was not okay to be me.

I tried to gain some weight so I wouldn't be known as the 'skinniest girl in class'. I wanted to look normal in my school uniform dress instead of wearing my school dress paired with trousers to cover my super skinny legs. I tried to gain weight so I could ditch the long sleeves I wore under my school shirt to hide my tiny arms. I changed my hairstyle to look cooler, and I also upgraded my wardrobe and started watching the TV channels other kids liked to watch in an attempt to fit in.

When I was eleven, I didn't feel like it was okay to be me — to show that nerdy part of me. When I was eleven, I was afraid of missing out, of not being invited to the birthday parties and not being a part of the dance performances. I was also afraid of having no one to share a meal with or hang out with after school if I continued to be that nerdy kid.

During the day, I tried to look cooler; but as soon as I arrived home, I removed that entire facade and went running back to my books. At home, I continued to secretly love my schoolbooks.

Sometimes I stayed after school to hang out with the cool kids the day before a test to prove to them that I was as cool as they were — and that I didn't care much about books. But those 'cool' afternoons often cost me some sleep... I would have to stay up that night studying for all I didn't read during the afternoon because, secretly, I still wanted the thrill of getting high grades.

The studious person in me was alive and well — well-hidden, that is... I was living a double life, and it was exhausting. Eventually, I mastered reflecting the values and behaviours of the cool kids in my day-to-day life so that I could be accepted. Disconnecting and reconnecting to my true identity was exhausting, but that was all I knew for a moment.

At one point, being liked became more important than being me. But I can tell you from experience that nobody can sustain a double life forever. Everyone seemed to admire me, *except me* (and that's not a very pleasant position to be in). At one point, the weight of disconnecting from my true identity became heavier and harder to bear than my desire to be liked by others.

By then, I had forgotten who I was. So, I had to peel off the layers that covered who I truly was.

As I began to peel off some layers, I felt some relief. As the layers started to show, not everyone was happy, but I continued to search for myself. Underneath those layers, I was searching for the me that was truly me — not the me that was perfect for others.

The truest version of ourselves lives somewhere within us. Some of our past choices may have caused us to put different types of wallpaper on ourselves to please those around us. As the years go by, we end up putting so many different layers of wallpaper on ourselves in order to keep up with everyone's latest expectations of us — only to find out that we have forgotten what our bare wall looks like. When you decide to take the journey back to yourself, you'll discover there isn't just one layer to peel off. There are many layers. And not everyone will like the raw and unpolished you. Yet, it is vital for you to see that raw and unpolished version of yourself.

To make sense of your world, you need to first meet the rawest and purest version of yourself — to see its beauty as well as its power — and be okay with it. I saw that version of myself on 2 November 2019; I accepted and embodied the rawest and purest version of myself without worrying about what others around me thought of it. After a series of exercises facilitated by one of my coaches, I stood on a chair in a country I had never been to. During an event I was attending for the first time, I used my voice to say something that was buried deep inside my heart. And from the depths of my heart and soul, I made this bold declaration:

'I'm ready to live in my brilliance'.

I stood in my power for the first time in a long time, unrecognisable to many but feeling totally like myself. I was comfortable in my own skin — for the first time in a long time.

You see, for years, I was afraid to express who I was. I was fearful of expressing who and what I longed to become. I was scared of being judged, and I was afraid of being excluded. With time, I've come to realise that our natural talents and gifts are best expressed when we live in our truths. When we allow our true selves to shine through, we begin moving towards living our truths. Lean into the possibility of travelling the journey back to yourself and watch the transformation that comes with your decision. Success loves to partner with the uniqueness that's inside of you, not what you think you should be to please others.

Opportunity to write

Below are some questions to help you take the first step towards the journey back to yourself. Grab a pen and paper and find a quiet spot. Ask your heart the following questions, and then journal your heart's answers.

▸ *What were you so afraid of that caused you to run away from yourself?*
▸ *Why were you so afraid to be yourself and live your truth?*
▸ *What did that fear lead to?*
▸ *Why are you still afraid today?*
▸ *What is it costing you to not be yourself?*
▸ *How do you wish to see yourself?*
▸ *How do you want others to see you?*
▸ *How can you reconnect with your true identity?*

Scan the QR code below
if you need to hear some words of encouragement:

CHAPTER 2

YOU HAVE NO IDEA HOW STRONG YOU ARE

The day I got a glimpse of what it feels like to 'stand in my power' was the moment I decided that I was done living a double life. I was done putting my true identity to sleep in order to be liked by others. I was done hiding the truest version of myself. I had enough of living in a world designed by others, and I wanted to live in a world designed by me.

There's a formula that can help you successfully design your own world. But before the formula can work, you need to understand your strengths. Before you design your world, you need to know you're strong enough to do it. Otherwise, the weak stories you hear from others or the ones you tell yourself will sabotage your world and weaken the formula.

For a long time, I didn't know how strong I was. Once I started to question whether I was strong enough to be the person I was born to be, life found various ways to show me my truth. One of the many ways I got to see my strength was when I met the man I love. I didn't let people's opinions of him influence me. I refused to let their vision of the type of guy I should date enter my world. I didn't let our cultural differences stand in our way.

Let me remind you that by the time I started dating the man I love, I had lost my true identity, yet with the tiny bit of strength I had left, I stood my ground. With what remained of my most authentic self, I stood up for the love we both shared, and I stood up for what I believed in.

Strength is your ability to stand up for what you believe in, even if no one else believes in it. Standing up for what you believe in often comes with its own set of consequences. As I stood up for the love I believed in, some people indirectly questioned my choice. Others told me to my face that it was only a matter of time before I would see that we were not a match. Yet, we continued to stand strong, learning and growing up together.

Months and years went by, but one thing remained true: he always encouraged me to be myself and be brave enough to become the person I was born to be. It took a while for me to have the courage to see the truest and rawest version of myself and to search for the person I was born to be. But he stood by my side (patiently and firmly) in my journey of self-discovery until I managed to find my long-lost identity.

Finding my identity wasn't a bright and straightforward journey. It was a dark time in my life. I lost my way so many times. Every time I took a wrong turn, the light on my path got a little dimmer. My confidence diminished, my finances suffered and my strength withered. My life felt grimmer with each passing day. Yet, my biggest cheerleader never stopped loving and encouraging me to find my truest identity, not even for a second. He seemed to have enough strength for us both. But his *seemingly* endless strength ended up costing him something — his health!

As time passed, I was still nowhere near finding, let alone living, my true identity. But that didn't stop him from being my biggest cheerleader. Even when I no longer had the strength to be his biggest cheerleader, he continued to be mine. Slowly but surely, he began to need encouragement too — but I had none to offer. As his biggest cheerleader failed to show up for him day in and day out, he buried himself a little deeper in his work. At one point, he was working sixteen-hour shifts every day of the week (including Sundays) because none of us knew better, and that cost him his health.

When you're so buried in your own darkness, it's easy to think everyone else has a better life than you. When you're travelling down that long, winding road, feeling sad and frustrated as you try but fail to reconnect with your true identity, you might unconsciously end up leading your loved ones to experience those dark feelings too.

I've had glimpses of who I was. And while those glimpses shaped my values, they were nowhere near strong enough to help me see my true identity. It took me twenty-nine years to clearly see who I am — to see the truest and rawest version of myself for the first time. Once I saw that version of myself, there was no going back, and I could no longer pretend to be the person everyone else wanted me to be. When you know exactly who you are, something magical happens! You begin to find strength in places you didn't even know existed to start or continue designing your own world.

A part of my world started to crumble as my partner's health deteriorated. As he fought for his life, it was my turn to step up. Thankfully, I had already caught a glimpse of who I was. And that glimpse of ourselves is all we need to access our strength. I found a strength in me that I didn't even know existed — an unknown force that enabled me to step into my toughest cheerleading role as he fought to recover his health.

After some long and arduous months with Stefan's declining health, we started to see some progress. With Stefan's health improving, he began feeling strong enough to start eating more varied foods and go for longer walks. Despite being physically active all my life, exercise felt like a foreign word to me because we had paused everything else to focus on improving his health condition. On a sunny summer day, I walked into a new gym to purchase a membership. That day felt like the first day of school. Having been away from the gym for over six months, I thought it would be a good idea for me to work with a trainer. I signed up for a session with a woman I had never met or heard of before. I didn't take the time to research the trainer, even though I tend to research my coaches thoroughly before opting in.

To this day, I don't know if that was grace or if our paths had to cross that year, but I showed up at the scheduled time and had the honour of meeting one of the strongest and most athletic women I've ever met in my life! She stood tall, with long brown hair, and every muscle wave on her well-defined body embodied strength! She greeted me with the kindest smile I'd seen in a while and said, 'Hello, good to meet you. Are you ready to train?' At that moment, I knew right away that she meant business! This woman was willing to revive all my hibernating muscles. We did a few exercises to test my strength levels and give her a better understanding of what our next training would look like.

Our first meeting was just a 'test training session' for her, but for me, it was the most intensive training session I've ever had in my life! In the middle of all the hard work and sweat, I had thoughts of self-doubt: *This is hard; I'm not sure I can do it. I think I'll pass out if I have to do one more rep.* But then she interrupted our training session to say something that shook me to my core!

She said, 'You have no idea how strong you are!' Having gone through a wild rollercoaster ride in pursuit of helping Stefan recover his health, I needed to hear those words. Her encouraging comment made so much sense to me! I know her words didn't make me any stronger, but hearing that from a person who barely even knew me — from a complete stranger who had no idea what Stefan and I had just been through in the last few months — was exactly what I needed to help me see my own strengths.

That day, Marina's encouragement helped me see my own strength. I don't take her words lightly. Whenever I find myself in a challenging situation, I tell myself the exact same words that she once shared with me: 'You have no idea how strong you are'. Just like finding the strength to do one more rep at the gym, those simple words of encouragement can help you find the strength you need to succeed in any of life's challenges.

You don't have to go through a near-death experience with a loved one in order to realise your strength. We all have strength, and we can all find the strength within — in places we don't even know existed. We all have the fortitude to design our own world. We just need to tap into that strength.

Believe me when I say this: there is strength inside you at this very moment and **you have no idea how strong you are.**

Opportunity to write

Below are some questions to help you reveal your strength. Grab a pen and paper and find a quiet spot. Ask yourself the following questions and journal your answers.

▸ *When was the last time you managed to get through a challenging situation?*
▸ *What were your thoughts before you managed to overcome that situation?*
▸ *What were your thoughts after you managed to overcome that challenging situation?*
▸ *What did you learn about yourself?*

CHAPTER 3

BE BRAVE ENOUGH TO TAKE A STAND AND ASK FOR WHAT YOU WANT

After I completed my A-levels in Mozambique, I knew for a fact that I wanted to continue my higher education in England — a country I had never visited but felt so drawn to. I had a soft spot for business studies, but there was a catch... My father was totally against the idea of having his youngest daughter living and studying in England all by herself.

When I first expressed my dream of attending university in England, his disapproval was clear and concise: 'No. England is too far, and it's too cold!' He was right about that, but I couldn't care less about the distance or the cold, which led me to give it another try. But this time, I was a bit more specific about what I wanted to study in England, hoping that my clarity would help him take my dream a bit more seriously. When I brought up the conversation to study management and international business in England, I finally received my second 'no'.

Anyone who knows my father knows that any further attempts to bring up the same conversation would mean trouble. You see, there isn't much room for compromise with my father's decisions. His military and engineering background makes him very firm and precise with his responses.

My father doesn't leave much room to entertain any further conversations. In other words, 'Dad's decisions' are pretty much final. Any 'good daughter' would be expected to put that study abroad idea to rest. But I couldn't do that. I knew I wanted this opportunity more than anything, and I had to find a way. I had to find some leverage, so I did!

My father had a friend who had lived in the UK for over ten years before moving back to Mozambique. Tio Zubaida, or Uncle Zubaida as I called him, also happened to be my eldest brother's wedding godfather. My brother's wedding took place in the same year that studying in the UK felt like a distant dream. As the family began working on my eldest brother's wedding preparations, Uncle Zubaida visited our house more frequently. Uncle Zubaida's children grew up in England and studied at British universities. Uncle Zubaida had deep insights about the UK, and my father had a deep respect for him. Bingo! I had found my leverage.

I approached Uncle Zubaida one afternoon to express that my wish to further my studies in the UK was being met with strong resistance from my father. When I asked him what life was like in the UK and why he supported his children's choice to study in the UK, Uncle Zubaida gave a beautiful account of life in the UK. He even showed me his daughter's graduation photo with a massive 'proud dad' grin on his face. I smiled back and asked him if he would consider helping me talk to my father. He jumped up from his seat, accepted the challenge and said, 'Let's do this, girl!'

Then and there, he walked straight to my father and asked for his reasons against studying in England. Wow! My heart skipped a beat for a minute. I didn't know Uncle Zubaida would be so direct with my father! He had a question in mind, and he was brave enough to ask without any hesitation. To my surprise, my father gave the most unexpected response ever.

I don't know if Uncle Zubaida's question caught my father by surprise, or if he knew his reasons weren't strong enough, but my father responded that he had nothing against me studying in England. Shortly after, my eldest brother joined the conversation. Uncle Zubaida gave them both one of the sincerest smiles I'd ever seen and reminded them that it would be unwise to stop a young girl who wanted to take her studies seriously.

Uncle Zubaida reminded them that I could end up making worse choices if I was left to feel unsupported when trying to pursue my dreams. My father looked me straight in the eyes and said he approved of my higher education in England. That day, I managed to turn his 'no' into a 'yes', simply because I was brave enough to take a stand and ask for what I wanted. And I got it! That moment was my 'Ask For What You Want 101' lesson.

To this day, I simply can't imagine where I would be now if I hadn't dared to ask Uncle Zubaida to speak to my father about studying in the UK. At times, I catch myself wondering what my life trajectory would have looked like if I had chickened out after my father's first 'no' and second 'no'. What would my life look like today?

As a result of my decision to study in the UK, I've had the opportunity to explore my potential. I've had the opportunity to study management, international business, and entrepreneurship in England's top universities. I've had the opportunity to embark on my own personal discovery journey. I've had the joy of working with thousands of students and graduates who are discovering their strengths and career paths. It is here that I've happily coached young adults on how to navigate the pressures of achieving personal success, improving their mental health and staying true to who they are. Here, I've had the blessing of partnering with other higher education providers to help university students make a smoother transition from university to graduate life. I've had the privilege of joining the board of advisors responsible for giving strategic advice and supporting the School of Business and Management at Royal Holloway University. I've worked with companies to train their interns and new hires to communicate effectively and deliver standout presentations. And it was here in the UK that I had the honour of meeting the bravest heart I know — Stefan.

I met Stefan in my first year at university through a mutual group of friends. Although we spent about an hour together, our lives took completely different paths until we met again in our second year and decided to stick together to this day. You see, Stefan has something that every great human being or movie character has — a brave heart. With his brave heart, I've watched him overcome insurmountable challenges. I've watched him soften the toughest people out there, and I've watched him win, not just once or twice. I've watched him win this game called designing your own world simply because he was brave enough to take a stand and ask for what he wanted.

I have to admit that there have been times when I thought, *Okay — there's no way he'll get that* or *He's going to annoy them by making such a request because he's asking for too much now.* Before Stefan purchased his first property investment, he had a specific budget in mind for a two-bedroom house on a popular street in Liverpool. When I first heard what he was prepared to pay, I shook my head and thought, *No way — that's a bit too much to ask!* How on earth was he planning to buy a house for ten per cent below market value?

Our thoughts differed in one very simple way. I didn't believe it was possible to purchase a house on that street for ten per cent below market value. On the other hand, Stefan believed it was totally possible, and he was willing to make it happen! When Stefan started negotiating the purchase of his first property, I watched the magic happen. I witnessed him connect with the seller. I heard him share his story with the property agent. And I watched him ask for the price he wanted to pay until he got it.

Time and time again, Stefan has been living proof that you can get what you ask for. Throughout the years, I've watched Stefan use his brave heart to ask for what he wanted, and I've watched him get what he wanted. At times, he got himself an even better deal than he had initially planned. Stefan had the bravery to ask for the price he wanted to pay for his first house, and he got it. He purchased his first buy-to-let house at ten per cent below market value.

Life will give you what you're brave enough to ask for. If you're not brave enough to ask for what you want, you won't be brave enough to take action, and you won't be brave enough to share your story.

When you begin to design your own world, you will need a brave heart to take a stand and ask for what you want. You will need to believe in what you're asking for, and at times, you will need to share your story. The formula to design your own world doesn't work if you are unwilling to share your story and ask for what you want.

CHAPTER 4

THE ONLY THING WORTH CHANGING IS YOUR PERSPECTIVE

The way we see things through our own lens shapes our views of the world. When it comes to shaping our world, it's important to remember that our experiences and the lesson attached to each experience cannot be fully understood without the full picture. The trouble is that the complete picture isn't always available early in the process.

The whole picture is released over time, and, sometimes, it is released slower than what our patience can bear. If (and when) we are open to seeing the complete picture, we finally get to see a new perspective. Once we see the complete picture, our perspective about a certain point in our lives can change.

Your complete picture can mean hope, when once upon a time, your incomplete picture meant hopelessness. Your full picture can replace fear with courage. Your complete picture can show you the lesson that you had to experience to redirect you to your mission. This new picture can help you understand that the only thing worth changing is your perspective (not others around you).

Your world will change when your perspective about yourself changes. My world changed when my perspective changed. When I opened myself up to see the entire picture that was in front of me, I was able to free myself from one specific limiting perspective. I was able to escape a limiting perspective that almost took me to the grave and stole my hope and courage for a moment. With the complete picture, I was finally able to see where the limiting perspectives about myself had led me and how incompatible that place was with the world I wished to design.

For years, I believed I was a failure. I felt unworthy. I lived in doubt. I doubted my present, I questioned my future and I doubted my abilities. The only view I had was a picture of regret, regretting my past mistakes and all the money I had invested to make my skincare and my haircare business work out. And then, I had nothing to show for my efforts. The regret I felt was not my full picture; it was only my narrow lens, but I didn't know better at the time. And so, I lived through that narrow lens for years.

I put my head down and accepted my narrow lens as if it were my full picture. I kept my head down because I didn't want to be hurt every time I looked up to see my present. For years, I lived with my head down. During that time, while my head was down, I didn't even realise that the full picture had unfolded — unfolded right in front of me. All I had to do was look up. But I was so terrified of looking up — I didn't dare!

Just like a child with a fresh bruise, I chose not to look at my wound. You know that pinch you feel in your heart after looking at a fresh bruise? And somehow, that pinch seems to go away when you're not looking at it because you're watching a YouTube video or doing something fun? And if by any chance you dare to look at your fresh bruise, the mere act of looking at it makes your heart pinch again! As you look at your bruise, you then realise how deep the cut is, and all the pain seems to flood back in. Don't you find it strange how the bruise didn't even feel like it was there when your head was looking in a different direction?

Most children know that if you look away from the bruise long enough, one day, you'll wake up and realise that your bruise is gone. And sometimes, not even a scar is left behind.

Getting your complete picture pretty much works the same way. The more you look through your narrow lens, the more it hurts, and all you can feel is pain. The pain of regret. The pain of failure. The pain of doubt. The pain of disappointment. The pain of hopelessness. But if you dare to look away from your lens for long enough, you'll soon realise that your narrow picture has unfolded into a full-blown picture. And the part of the picture that used to hurt you has either evolved into something better or is no longer there.

When I dared to look at the full picture that had unfolded right in front of me, I realised that my first business venture, TSAKA, was a lesson I had to learn. TSAKA was an important lesson that taught me in what circumstances the formula doesn't work. At first, I couldn't believe that what I called my 'failed experiences with TSAKA' no longer carried the same weight. With this new insight, the pinch in my heart was gone, and I could finally see the lesson and stand strong in my power. As I stood in my power, my perspective about myself and my world changed.

The moment I changed my perspective about TSAKA and myself, I lifted a burden off my shoulders and resumed life with a new outlook that enabled me to live and love the world I was designing.

Some may wonder what happens to us when we're too afraid to look at the entire picture. Well, the answer is that we continue to live through the narrow lens and we miss the lessons and the opportunity to design our own world. We miss the opportunity to heal from our failures, and then release them. Take the time you need to find the courage to look at the whole picture that has unfolded in front of you. Dare to look at the full picture and see the perspective that's in front of you — a perspective that is ready to give you the hope, freedom and courage to live and love the world you design.

CHAPTER 5

FILLING THE GAP

In retrospect, my biggest mistakes often came from a place of setting the next big goal without fully taking stock of my current situation. Time and time again, I chose to turn a blind eye to where I was and how I felt about it. Instead, I just rushed to set my next goal!

Taking stock of your current situation isn't easy — especially when things haven't gone according to plan. Not many people have the courage to sit with themselves and look at their undesired situation square in the face — to explore the feelings that come with living in an undesired now.

It's so much easier to find a goal to give you new hope for a better tomorrow instead of having that honest conversation with your now (your current situation). I was that person. But, at that time, I didn't know that before you reach out to set a new goal, you need to fill the gap first. Leave no gap unattended because sooner or later the gap will show, and you'll find yourself living in your new, undesired result.

Filling the *gap* between where you are and where you want to be is a much-needed exercise when designing your own world. It's a milestone that you cannot avoid or skip. There's no point implementing the formula or attempting to design your own world without first filling the *gap* between where you are now and where you want to be.

In order to get to where you want, first you need to know where you are. The formula will not work if you don't know where you are now.

Don't you find it helpful when the GPS tells you your exact location and then maps out your options to get to your desired destination? Depending on how close or far you are to your desired destination, you may need to add in some extra time for an overnight stay, to take a break, to refuel or take a different route to avoid congestion. Or you may even choose a more efficient method of travel altogether.

When you avoid looking at your current situation, it's a lot like deciding to walk instead of driving towards your desired destination that's equivalent to a twelve-hour walk. Simply thinking about where we want to be won't always reveal what we must do to achieve our goals.

With that in mind, take some time to reflect on your life by answering the questions below.

Opportunity to write

- ▸ *What are you proud of?*
- ▸ *What is your biggest achievement?*
- ▸ *What is your greatest regret?*
- ▸ *What don't you like about your life at this present moment?*
- ▸ *Why are you reading this book?*
- ▸ *What are you looking to find in this book?*

Remember, what you're good at and what you love doing are two different things. What you love doing sets your soul on fire, and you have it within you already.

- ▸ *When you were a child, you were probably exposed to something that set your soul on fire. What was it?*
- ▸ *How do you feel about your finances?*
- ▸ *How do you feel about your health?*

▶ *How do you feel about your body?*

▶ *How do you feel about your friends?*

▶ *How do you feel about your family?*

▶ *How do you feel about the work that you do?*

▶ *But most importantly, how do you feel about yourself and where you are now?*

In the following chapters, I will share a formula to help you bridge the gap between where you are and where you want to be. This formula will help you design the world you want to live in.

Please don't skip the questions in this chapter because the formula won't work if you don't understand where you are now. I recommend you grab a notebook and write the answers to all fourteen questions before moving on to the next chapter. Running doesn't necessarily mean arriving. Please take the time to write down the answers to all the questions in this chapter.

I used to be that person who bought books to learn something new. Trouble was, I'd read all about the action I had to take, then put off the action for another day. Days became months, and all I was left with was information (not results).

You cannot go from here to there without doing the necessary work. How you feel in this moment will guide you into the next moment. Before you can fill in any gaps in your life, you need to understand where you are now. As painful or difficult as it may be to take stock of your current situation, it is a much-needed exercise that helps you focus on the now, not the excuses.

If you dare to look at your current situation, you may or may not find something you don't want to see and have been trying to avoid. Sometimes, the easiest way to understand what you do want is by becoming crystal clear on what you don't want. Don't let anyone fool you into thinking that you can ignore where you are now and run along to pick where you want to be.

At one point, I remember signing up for a £9,000 online course simply because I saw several video testimonials of successful students from around the world who were making a minimum of £10,000 a month after taking that course. I watched a webinar and countless testimonials, and thought to myself, *Wow! That could be me!* I bought into the promise of increased income without first looking at my current situation square in the face. And without understanding who I was and what the most authentic version of myself looked like.

If I had completed the exercise in this chapter and taken the time to reflect on my own situation first, I know for a fact that I would not have paid that price tag only to realise that what I'd bought into had nothing to do with what I was good at and what I loved doing. If I had answered the fourteen questions in this chapter, before I committed to that 'no refunds' course, I would have realised that the course I had planned to buy was in no shape or form allowing me to express the truest version of myself (not to mention that such an investment would undeniably end up putting a strain on my personal finances).

When you don't know where you are, it is easier for you to fall for a fancy social media advertisement or a promise for a better life 'if only you buy' this or that specific product or service. Instead of hoping that someone else's promise of a better life will work for you, why not have the conversation that you need to have with yourself, which is long overdue, and answer the questions I posed in this chapter? Then you can decide what your next best step is.

Remember, you're in control of your GPS. When you know where you are, you can always reroute to your desired destination — the world you design. When you know where you are now, the ability to design your own world moves closer to your fingertips. If you haven't already done so, go back and answer the questions in this chapter. You deserve to know where you are. And when you do, the road ahead will look so much clearer.

CHAPTER 6

YOU HAVE THE POWER

This is a very important chapter. If you skipped the exercise in the last chapter, do yourself a favour, go back to Chapter 5 and answer all fourteen questions. Once you know where you are, you have the power to choose where you want to be.

After you have identified where you are now, you have the power to choose a new destination that honours who you are. The only disclaimer here is that where you want to be must allow you to stay loyal to who you truly are. Choosing a new destination isn't about being seen in a certain way, and it's not about making someone else's dreams come true. Your new destination is not about making your parents proud, impressing your friends or pleasing society by doing what they expect of you. This new destination has nothing to do with expectations or disappointments. If you are dissatisfied with where you are now, you owe it to yourself to choose where you want to be. Dissatisfaction with where you are now, plus inaction, often results in wasted potential.

Choosing a new destination is all about honouring the truest version of yourself. It's about allowing yourself to live in your truest expression. And when you do that, you allow others to embrace their lives and live in their truest expression too.

You are not stuck. What if all you had to do was take the first step? What if all you had to do was make a commitment that from this day onward you're moving to a new destination that honours who you truly are? What if you could send yourself an SMS saying exactly where you wish to be, and then you could magically be there?

- ▶ *Would you do it?*
- ▶ *Would you send the SMS?*
- ▶ *What if the only person in this world who could send that SMS is you?*
- ▶ *Would you do it?*

If where you want to be does not allow you to stay loyal to yourself by honouring who you truly are, then pick a new destination, because you cannot sustain a lie forever. The formula I will share with you will *not* work if where you want to be does not honour who you truly are. If where you want to be does not allow you to express your truest self, then please pick a new destination. I've made the mistake of choosing a destination that did not honour who I truly was. Not once, not twice, but many times!

Initially, it was exciting to receive my first pay cheque. To be on holiday and still get paid. To tell my friends and family that a reputable organisation had employed me. To wake up, go to work and do my best. Initially, I felt lucky that I had chosen a new destination and felt accepted. (Whether we like to admit it or not, we all want to belong somewhere.)

Then, I began to see how my chosen destination did not allow me to be me. I began to realise that if I was serious about keeping that job, I would have to dim the parts of me that I loved the most.

In that job, they expected me to shine less than the people who had worked there longer. I had to be okay with having my ideas rebranded by my seniors and presented as theirs. Having understood the working code, first I blended in with simpler clothes and less bright colours. Then I tried to sound more like everyone else whenever I was given the opportunity to speak — whether that was in front of one person or four hundred people. And quite frankly, that to me was the hardest part. I've always loved telling stories and using my experiences to uplift and spread hope to different audiences. Although my natural height tells a different story about me, I've always loved the feeling of growing — anyone who knows me can confirm that I have the tendency to look for new ways to develop myself.

When I picked my new destination, I didn't realise that my strengths (the things that energise me the most) were not welcome in my new destination. I could use some of it, but not too much (or at least not as frequently as I would have loved to), because it would upset my colleagues. There's this funny thing that happens: when you're not allowed to be yourself, and you can only do the things you love the most in secret, a piece of you dies every day.

After I became more aware of my new destination, my initial excitement faded away. Minutes began to feel like hours at work, and everything started to feel like an act. The way I behaved had to match the features of my new destination, and it was exhausting to live in that lie from Monday to Friday.

My weekends felt like a required detoxification session just to look and behave according to the standards at work the following week.

Do you know how sad it is to live in a new destination when everyone else assumes you are happy there? To hear from your loved ones how proud they are because you work in such a prestigious place?

Whatever destination you choose for yourself, you're the only one who has to be content with your choice to live there. No words or compliments can ever lift the burden off your shoulders if you choose to live in a destination that does not allow you to live the truest version of yourself. No smile or feeling of pride expressed by a loved one is worth the sacrifice of not honouring who you truly are. That's why your new destination needs to come from a place of truth, and it must allow you to stay loyal to yourself by honouring who you truly are.

If your strength is negotiating, and you love to negotiate deals and speak to people, then picking a new destination that puts you in an environment of negotiating might not be enough. Now, stop and take a moment, and imagine that you have secured a job that deals with company mergers and acquisitions (M&A) — a lot of negotiating happens behind the scenes before the deal is actually signed off. Exciting, right? Imagine that your role in this M&A company involves compiling data for the company negotiators to make sense of before they start negotiating the merger or acquisition (without you!).

Imagine that your everyday work revolves around crunching numbers that will be used for important negotiations. And although you have the skills to negotiate, and you have watched your peers make some mistakes in the negotiation process, your input is not welcome! And the few times you've tried to get involved, you were politely asked to not interfere. Imagine living in the proximity of something you love doing but not being able to do it? Not so exciting, right?

It's not enough to choose a new destination. Your new goal needs to allow you to express your truest self (and not pretend you enjoy what you do when in reality you wished you were doing something else — that you know for a fact you can and love to do).

We can all survive in a destination that doesn't honour who we truly are. But trying to survive is not the same thing as designing your own world. To design your own world means choosing a destination that honours who you truly are — to use your spark instead of hiding it. Because your spark is powerful, your spark has the power to bring light to someone else's life and inspire them to design their own world too — in a way that honours who they truly are.

You always had the power!

You have everything you need to take yourself there — to design your own world. You just need to be brave enough and strong enough to choose. You are not stuck!

For two years, I thought I was stuck, but that was before I realised that I had the power. When I believed that I was stuck, I had all the evidence to prove that I was stuck in my destination — that I basically had no choice and couldn't design a new destination. Fortunately, I eventually came to a realisation that changed my life for the better. I discovered a formula that positively changed my world, and that's why I'm writing this book: to share that same formula with you. I won't rush into sharing the formula quite yet, because it works best when you have more awareness of self. And besides, there are a few more messages that I need to share with you first.

For now, I'll leave you with this thought:

You have the power to create and
design the world you want to live in,
or let your world be designed by others!
Are you willing to use your power?

CHAPTER 7

SET YOURSELF FREE

Set yourself free of shame,
blame, guilt and regret.

We all have our fair share of shame, blame, guilt and regret. Whether it's a shame that comes from using our power, the blame for not using our power, the guilt of what we could have done with our power or the pain of regret that comes with all the above, we all experience these feelings.

I experienced shame when I was on track to rank as the second top student in my class, was nominated global ambassador and had received a university award, recognising my outstanding contributions; yet, when I went to bed at night, the only thing I could think about was how much of a hard time I was having securing a full-time job in my final year of university.

On the surface, I had accomplished what most students only wish to achieve. I had the high grades and the recognition. At my fingertips, I had the 'news' that would make most parents proud. But I didn't share the news with them because I was heavily burdened with shame. All the awards and accolades meant nothing at the time, because for a brief moment, I actually believed I had all the odds stacked against me to secure a full-time job after graduation.

Time and time again, I met with academics and lecturers, who reassured me that it was normal not to get hired as an international student. These same people claimed that my chances of securing a full-time job were very slim because I needed a visa sponsorship. I was encouraged to face the reality that priority was first given to UK and EU citizens. And if by any chance a suitable candidate was not found for the job post, only then would the job offer be extended to an international passport holder. And the chances of that happening were very slim.

Early careers recruiters told me that if I had graduated in 2007, I would have had a much better chance of securing a full-time job after graduation because of the post-study working visa that would have allowed me to stay in the UK for two years to look for a job after graduation.

People who were more intelligent and more qualified than I was looked me straight in the eyes and told me, 'To avoid disappointment, you should start making arrangements to return to your home country by October 2014.'

At around the same time, my international friends at university continued to confirm this same rhetoric during the second term of our final year. They told me that they had tried everything, but they could not find a job. And they warned me that if they couldn't secure a full-time job after interning at top multinational companies like Yahoo and Deloitte, then there was no chance I would secure a full-time job either. In other words, I should pack my bags and leave. I didn't have those big company names on my CV, and for a moment, their reasoning made sense. But for one reason or another, I just couldn't fully believe all these stories I heard. I knew I needed to search for the best London to Maputo flight deals. But every time I opened my laptop to begin the search, my mind wandered, and I thought about all kinds of possibilities.

Even though I didn't have the big names on my CV, deep inside, I believed I was worthy of a full-time job. Deep inside, I had faith. Faith that I had what it took to secure a full-time job in the UK after graduation — if, and only if, I could get past the online application systems that would cold-heartedly disqualify my application before I even had the chance to apply. I had to find a way to show my worth first. I had to make my application land first, and then have the working visa sponsorship conversation later.

As much as I wanted to submit my online application, ticking a pre-application box confirming that I needed a working visa often meant I couldn't even make it to the job application page, let alone submit my application. Thankfully, I eventually woke up from that brief period of doubt when I thought, *I can't do this.*

When I set myself free of that shame, I stopped blaming my passport and the fact that I needed a visa. I let go of the guilt and regret I had for not working on internships earlier, and I focused on my desired result. I stopped thinking about what others thought I could or could not achieve, and I got really specific about the result I wanted from this experience. When you believe in your core that your desired result will help give you the freedom to express who you truly are, then the formula will work.

The formula will work in your favour when you believe your desired result supports your freedom to be the person you know you are inside. In my case, my desired result was securing a full-time job within the consulting industry after graduation. I took bold, strategic marketing steps to achieve my career goals by creating an evening networking event with the intention of putting a group of prospective employers in the same room to share my story and my dream of working in the consulting industry. I invited ten decision-makers working in the consulting firms I wanted to work for. Nine out of ten responded positively to my invitation and showed up at the networking event.

I invited MBA students and undergraduates to meet these nine consultants and also to celebrate the winner of a cold-calling competition I had organised earlier that month. I invited some lecturers, who happily championed the networking event and sponsored the catering.

That evening, I demonstrated various skills that no number of paragraphs on my CV could have accurately described. Everyone attending the event (including the nine potential employers) witnessed my public speaking, communication, project management, stakeholder management and event management skills.

I believed in my desired result with all my strength. I believed I deserved to achieve my goals, and I believed my desired result was a platform that would open doors for me to express who I truly was. The formula worked like magic!

That evening, I walked away with one consulting job offer and a business card to arrange a meeting with their team. Walking home that evening felt so magical. I'm not entirely sure I walked home. It felt more like flying because I finally had my foot in the door! After months of rejection emails and rejected applications, I breathed in a sigh of relief, knowing that I had achieved my desired result of working full-time in a management consulting company.

The following day, another one of the nine prospective employers came to one of my lectures to offer me a job at his consulting firm. I thanked him for his time but broke the news that I had already accepted a job offer the previous night. To my surprise, employer number two kept in touch via email for the next two weeks — trying to match the salary offer of the other company — but I had already decided to work for employer number one.

Looking back on it now, this was the second time I had (unconsciously) put the formula to work, and it worked perfectly. The craziest thing about this entire experience where I (unconsciously) put the formula to work was that employer number one didn't even have a visa sponsorship in the first place. After witnessing my work and skills in action at the networking event, their company was willing to get a UK work licence (also known as a UK Tier 2 visa licence) just to hire me, and I was the first non-UK and non-EU employee they hired. I share this experience to remind you that your desired result is possible even when you have all the odds stacked against you!

Before you try to achieve a desired result, set yourself free of those negative emotions. There's freedom in setting yourself free of shame, blame, guilt and regret. Give yourself the gift of freedom to design your own world and express the person you were born to be.

CHAPTER 8

YOU CANNOT CHEAT YOURSELF

You can cheat anyone else but yourself.

You cannot cheat yourself and design your own world at the same time. All the accolades, the awards and the education mean nothing if you don't take the journey back to yourself and stay loyal to who you truly are. If you are not letting the person you were born to be express himself or herself, then you are cheating yourself!

It's okay if you have cheated yourself before. There is no need to have any shame, blame, guilt and regret. You didn't know better at the time — you probably didn't even know who you truly were at that time. What is not okay, though, is to cheat yourself after you know who you truly are!

Deep down, we all know who we truly are. Some of us just choose to ignore the truth of who we really are and want to be. You choose to ignore that part of you that makes you *you* because you don't want to upset or disappoint someone else. When we do that, it's as if we're stabbing ourselves in the back every day. And sooner or later, you lose touch with yourself. You lose the ability to design your own world and end up living like a zombie (or even worse, a puppet), aimlessly following everyone else's commands or letting someone else design your own world.

I don't say this to mock anyone. I've been there myself. Let me tell you about a time in my life when I cheated myself — not once, but twice — one after the other...

After securing my full-time job in consulting, a year later, the job no longer felt right for my life. The thrill of my new role had worn off, and I found myself pretending to be happy and that I wanted to be there, even pretending that I aspired to be like the CEO one day.

I was dissatisfied with where I was, and I was clearly cheating myself. But instead of taking the journey back to myself and using my power to pick a new destination that honoured who I truly was,

I behaved as if I had opened this book, ignored all the pages and skipped right into Chapter 6! Without much reflection or thought, I decided to pick a new destination as soon as I realised that I was dissatisfied with where I was. I didn't take the time to understand who I was, why I was dissatisfied and what got me there.

Instead, I woke up one day and decided to be an entrepreneur. I chose to be an entrepreneur because I thought that would make my parents proud. I believed that would impress my friends. I thought that was what society expected of me. Since I was an 'A student', I felt I also had to prove I was smart enough to be an entrepreneur. And that's when I cheated myself for the second time.

On that occasion, my goal was to be a successful skincare entrepreneur, so I started a company called TSAKA. I chose that name without even realising that the meaning of the word TSAKA would take on added significance during the next three years of my life.

TSAKA in the Ronga dialect of Mozambique means 'happiness'. And that word pretty much sums up what happened to me in the next three years. During my TSAKA years, I was basically searching for my happiness. The trouble was that I was trying to design my world *without* first connecting to who I truly was.

I started by launching a product. Every business has something to sell, right? In my case, my company sold a face mask.

It was a natural and preservative-free anti-inflammatory mask with soothing plant extracts from a rare African plant that visibly reduces the appearance of hyperpigmentation. The mask had instant results, lots of history and countless stories to tell. So, I took all the strategic marketing steps to launch it. I imported the raw materials from my home country, which made me feel great, because I was helping local farmers with the intention of placing larger orders in the future and hopefully making a difference in their lives.

I carefully worked on the packaging and quality of the product until I was satisfied with the look and feel of the product. Shortly after, with the support of its users, the face mask made its way to various media outlets. My face mask looked successful on paper.

The stories about the brand and me looked great on paper, but somehow it didn't feel right! I felt a disconnect. And even though I chose to ignore this disconnect, that feeling of disconnection simply wouldn't fade away. Initially, I thought it was probably Miss Impostor Syndrome playing mind games with me. But I now know it was not Miss Impostor Syndrome at all.

There was a discrepancy between the stories I told the world and the stories I told myself. To the world, I was a skincare entrepreneur. Deep down in my heart I didn't feel the same way. And sure enough, the formula didn't work, and I didn't get my desired result of being a successful skincare entrepreneur.

So, I tried again! And I stumbled on the same mistake — once again. Instead of taking the journey back to myself first, in order to understand who I truly was, I skipped Chapters 1–5, once again, and decided to pick a new destination. My new destination was more closely aligned to a product I felt closer to. Anyone who knows me knows that I love beautiful, strong and healthy hair. So, my next product choice seemed pretty obvious — a hair mask!

This time, I felt more connected to the product. Once again, I put together the best of my haircare abilities to use. I mixed and matched the best and most effective natural ingredients that have proved to work well on afro and curly hair.

I took all the strategic marketing steps to launch the product and shared my top haircare tips in the process.

My desired result was to create a successful natural haircare brand, which I did 'on paper'. Bloggers, influencers and everyone else told amazing stories about the product and the brand with no paid sponsorship. But every time I spoke about how successful my haircare brand was, I felt a disconnect. Again!

I enjoyed sharing the success stories about my TSAKA haircare brand, and for a moment, I was also excited about its initial success. But whenever I went to bed at night and thought about TSAKA's future, I felt a disconnect. Although everyone else seemed convinced that it was only a matter of time before TSAKA became a successful haircare brand, I didn't truly believe that I could reach that level of success with my haircare products. But since I was making some money, I tagged along with others on the idea of TSAKA being a highly successful haircare company one day. Deep down in my heart, though, I didn't really believe in those stories. And sure enough, TSAKA's haircare products did not grow to become a highly successful haircare brand! Although my new destination was more closely aligned to a product that I felt closer to, it still wasn't the truest expression of myself!

The formula didn't work, and I didn't get my desired result. This and other experiences made me realise that the formula to design your own world will only work when you have these three conditions present:

1. *Choose a specific result that honours who you are, then take bold, strategic marketing steps in the direction of your desired result.*

2. *Align your inner conversation with the stories you tell others.*

3. *Believe in your core that you deserve to get your desired result. To believe means to fully believe in the stories you tell others about yourself and your desired result.*

When you meet these three conditions, the formula can and will work to assist you in achieving your desired result. I rushed to implement the formula by picking a new destination twice without first taking the journey back to myself (to understand who I truly was), and it didn't bring me my desired result. Hence, the formula didn't work.

To be fair, the questions in Chapter 5 didn't even cross my mind. I didn't think of filling in the gaps before picking a new destination; I just chose a new destination because my current destination didn't feel good at the time. I was living in a world of expectations and disappointments because I had no idea who I was, and things only got worse because I wasn't willing to do the work. It takes courage to do the exercises in Chapter 5.

Few people have the courage to sit with themselves and look at their current situation and explore the feelings that come with living an undesirable present. It's so much easier to find a goal to give you new hope for a better tomorrow instead of having that honest conversation with your now (your current situation). I was that person. But what I didn't know then was that before you reach out for a new goal, you need to fill the gap first. Leave no gap unattended because, sooner or later, you'll find yourself living in your new, undesired experience.

Once we can see the full picture — our perspective about a certain point in our lives can change. I no longer see cheating myself twice in a row as a failure. It took a while for me to have the courage to look at those two moments square in the face. But once I did, I was able to see the truest and rawest version of myself and pick a destination that honours who I truly am.

When designing your world, I recommend you follow the chapters in this book in the same order as they appear here. Because you cannot realise how strong you are, be brave enough to take a stand, ask for what you want, change your perspective and fill in any gap without *first* knowing who you truly are. When you know who you are, you will pick your new destination. You will see the world you deserve to live in, and you will do everything in your power to design that world.

Now that you have understood in what circumstances the formula works, you are ready to learn about a formula that can help you achieve your desired results.

CHAPTER 9
BELIEVE IN YOURSELF

*It's never too late to believe in yourself,
to believe in who you are and the strength
that lives within you.
It's never too late to be brave and shift any
perspective that doesn't serve you well.
It's never too late to believe that you have
the power to design your own world!*

Regardless of everything you've been through, it's never too late to believe in yourself. There was a time in my life when I didn't believe in my own strength. My belief in my own strength and abilities went from 100 per cent to 1 per cent. At that time, I blamed my circumstances and people for not being where I wanted to be. I held on to that perspective without realising that by affirming those thoughts day in and day out, a part of my own self-belief died each day. And that lack of self-belief almost destroyed me.

It's easy to think that you are unlucky or that someone else had an easier life or was more supported than you — in order to justify where you are today. Just because it's easy to feel that way doesn't mean it serves you well. It takes courage to be brave and to shift any perspective that doesn't serve you well. One of the worst things you can do when designing your own world is to feed yourself with disempowering conversations that often begin with the words 'I can't'.

Once you decide to take the journey back to yourself in order to understand who you truly are, a spark within you lights up — a spark that was always there but wasn't given enough space to become a full-blown flame. With an awakened self-awareness, unconsciously, you start replacing your 'I can't' conversations with 'You know what? Maybe I can do this'. And eventually, your spark becomes a flame strong enough to light up your world.

When you realise who you are, you will discover how strong you are, you will be brave enough to take a stand for what you believe in and you will be more than willing to replace any perspective that doesn't empower you to design your own world. This is when your brilliant flame has the power to ignite anyone who comes near you.

When you believe that you have the power to design your own world, you will no longer believe that someone else can withhold your good from you. You will stop believing that someone out there needs to come and save you. You will no longer seek validation from others, and you will feel it in your core that your desired result is possible.

Throughout this book, I speak about a formula that will help you design your own world. This formula is so simple that it might even put some people off. But don't let its simplicity stop you from implementing it. It's called the SMS Formula.

Strategic Marketing + Storytelling

=

Results

I'll break it down for you. Strategic Marketing refers to creative and strategic plans executed to achieve your desired result.

Storytelling consists of two parts:
Storytelling = the stories we tell others + the stories we tell ourselves.

The secret ingredient to making this formula work is belief. A weak SMS lacks belief in at least one element of the formula — be it the strategic marketing plan, the stories you tell others or the stories you tell yourself. Throughout this book, I've shared some examples of weak SMSs.

I'll recap those stories once again to help you connect the dots.

Example 1: I *did not* believe in my strategic marketing plan, even though I did have a fair amount of belief in the stories I told others and the stories I told myself. This, in turn, contributed to my undesired result. During my final year at university, my career goal was to secure a full-time job. However, there was a time when I didn't believe in my initial strategic marketing plan. Initially, my strategic marketing plan consisted of submitting over fifty online job applications four months before I graduated to give myself enough time to secure a full-time job before my student visa expired.

One month of trying was enough to make me realise that my application was being disqualified before I even had the chance to complete the online job application process. When I realised that my strategic marketing plan of online applications was flawed, I stopped believing in that strategic marketing plan to help me secure a full-time job offer in management consulting. I knew for a fact that if I continued down that route of online applications, it would be tough to bypass the initial questionnaire that asked for my name, age, nationality and right to work in the UK. Every rejection I faced strengthened my sense of doubt.

And sure enough, I didn't achieve my career goal. Even though there were times when the stories I told myself about securing a full-time job went from, *I know I can do this* to *Well, maybe they're right*, I thought, *Maybe I can't secure a full-time job without interning in top multinational companies like Yahoo and Deloitte*. Maybe it was time to make the flight arrangements to travel back to Mozambique at the end of my course. Maybe there was no chance I would secure a full-time job with my current non-EU/non-UK passport.

Somewhere deep down in my heart, the greater part of me still had faith in achieving my career goal — if only I continued to try a different strategic marketing plan. And I did. I created a new strategic marketing plan that bypassed the online job application system and fast-tracked the application process by placing myself right in front of nine potential consulting company CEOs, who I strongly believed could be my potential employer.

This time around, I believed in my strategic marketing plan. I believed it when I told others that I would secure a full-time job within the UK management consulting industry. And most importantly, I believed the stories I told myself — that I wanted to secure and would secure a full-time job within the consulting industry. The SMS Formula worked like magic, and I secured a position at a UK boutique management consulting firm.

Example 2: I believed in my strategic marketing plan, but I *did not* fully believe in the stories I told others, and I *did not* believe in the stories I told myself. This, in turn, contributed to my undesired result. Having a solid strategic marketing plan that you believe in is a great starting point for achieving your desired result. But it's not enough to have a strategic marketing plan and believe in that plan. Once you start taking action to achieve your goals, the stories you tell yourself and the stories you tell others can either assist you or limit your success.

When I launched my face mask, my desired result was to be an entrepreneur. I had a strategic marketing plan, which I wholeheartedly believed in. So, I took all the strategic marketing steps to launch the face mask. I carefully tested and worked on the packaging and quality of the product until I was satisfied with it.

Shortly after, with the support of its users, the face mask made its way to various media outlets. You could almost say I had achieved my desired result of being an entrepreneur here. As a result of implementing the strategic marketing plan, the stories about the brand and I looked great on paper. However, there was still a discrepancy between the stories I told the world and the stories I told myself. I was an entrepreneur to the world, but deep down in my heart, I didn't believe I was a skincare entrepreneur, even as I forced myself to tell the world I believed I was on my way to becoming a successful one.

To the world, I was a successful skincare entrepreneur, but that did not match my definition of honouring who I truly was. As a result, I could not get myself to believe that I would become that person. And sure enough, the SMS Formula didn't work, and I didn't get my initial desired result of being a successful skincare entrepreneur.

Example 3: I believed in my strategic marketing plan and believed in the stories I told others. However, I *did not* believe in the stories I told myself. This, in turn, contributed to my undesired result. After realising I didn't believe in my initial goal to become a skincare entrepreneur, I thought I'd give entrepreneurship another try with hair care.

Since my early teen years, I've been good at caring for my hair and caring for other people's hair (as long as they allowed me to). At the time, though, I didn't know that there's a massive difference between being good at something and absolutely loving something. And because I had no clear understanding of those differences, I decided to create a successful natural haircare brand, which I did actually achieve, but only 'on paper'.

On paper, there was enough buzz from bloggers, influencers and everyone who tried and loved my hair products. This time around, I also enjoyed telling others about my TSAKA hair care, and I bought into its success. Although everyone else was pretty much sold on the idea that TSAKA's haircare products would become a success, the reality was, I didn't truly believe it. I believed in my strategic marketing plan, and it worked — I was enjoying the fruits of my labour, so I tagged along with TSAKA's initial haircare success.

However, underneath that initial success was a deeply rooted belief that I was not the one to take TSAKA to its next level of success. Sure enough, in the end, TSAKA's hair care did not grow to reach a new level of success! Although my new destination was more closely aligned with a product that I felt more passionate about, hair care still wasn't the truest expression of myself.

If you want to achieve anything less than your desired result, then one sure way to do so is to replace belief with doubt, in any of the three parts of this SMS Formula. But I must point out that it's pretty tough to force yourself into believing that your desired results will help you express the truest version of yourself, if you don't honestly believe it in your heart of hearts. Unless you genuinely believe that your desired result will help you express the truest version of yourself, you will inevitably doubt the stories you tell yourself, even if you are a skilled storyteller.

You can achieve your desired result with a lot more ease whenever you mix belief into every part of this SMS Formula, as I did in the latter part of Chapter 7. Once I believed in my new strategic marketing plan to secure my full-time job after graduation and also believed in the stories I told others (and myself), the SMS Formula finally worked!

Everything you see around you is a result of someone else designing their own world. Someone once had the dream of flying a plane. They believed in the strategic steps to execute that desired result + they believed in the stories they told themselves + they believed in the stories they told others about their desired result of travelling with wings = they achieved their desired result of flying an aeroplane, which also allows us to travel with wings. Even though we can't fly ourselves, we can travel in planes in the sky because someone else achieved their goal.

The few people out there who chose to design their own world have already understood this formula. They've understood the importance of mixing belief with every single part of this formula. Most importantly, they have implemented the SMS Formula to achieve their desired result.

When you picked up this book, something deep inside of you was longing to explore the possibility of designing your own world.

And now you know how.

CHAPTER 10

YOUR GAME PLAN

You're exactly where you are meant to be at this point in time to design your own world. You are not late. You are not lagging behind. You are not missing out. Please stop beating yourself up because you feel you 'should' have this or that by now — that grade, that job, that car, that house, the money and the award will eventually catch up with you. Please believe this in your heart of hearts.

Wipe your tears and find comfort in your heart, knowing that you are exactly where you need to be. All that hasn't worked out until now hasn't worked out for a good reason, and that's okay. Perhaps you didn't know better back then, but now you do. And the time has come for you to take responsibility for your game plan!

Now that you know what the SMS Formula is and how it works, I have a few words of caution.

Caution 1:

Be sure to treat it like a game — a strategic game with an *action plan*. It's a plan that honours who you truly are and what you believe in. The destination you want to reach is one of many destinations in your life's journey. It isn't the final destination. There's no need to burn yourself to exhaustion as you crawl, walk, run or fly towards your desired destination. Take care of your energy. Protect your heart and feed your mind with loving words of encouragement as you head towards your desired destination.

Caution 2:

The quickest way to get to your desired result is to follow your game plan and have fun along the way. The longest way to get to your desired result is to obsess about your game plan by questioning, day in and day out, why you haven't arrived at your new destination yet. Learn how to trust your own perfect timing because whenever we focus on what we don't have, where we want to be starts to feel further and further away from us.

Caution 3:

Your obsession with obtaining your desired result and designing your own world could also be your downfall. There may be moments when you will want to design your own world at all costs! Even if it costs you your happiness, your health and your good relationships. Whenever you find yourself in that position, remember who you are. Know who you are and what you believe in. Then trust your game plan and ignore any temptations to cut corners.

Caution 4:

The SMS Formula works best whenever you apply belief to all three parts of the formula and also choose to honour who you truly are. If you're only using the formula to achieve your desired result, then you may unintentionally end up designing a world of darkness, and you will soon realise the dullness of the world you created.

You will realise that there's no thrill in simply achieving a goal. Remember why you came here —

achieving your desired result was never about you or being proud, or making anyone else proud! Remember, your game plan is yours to play. The real fun of achieving your desired result lies in your ability to enjoy the journey. You must be willing to use the SMS Formula as if it were a game. You must be willing to play the SMS Formula game strategically and actually enjoy the game.

If you want to achieve your goals at a faster pace and also have fun along the way, you'll be there before you know it! You have a game plan — use it! Use it as a torch to light your path as you work towards achieving your desired results. And your torch may also light up someone else's path.

You have a game plan — use it!

CHAPTER 11

YOU ARE BECOMING

*You're on your way to becoming all
you were meant and want to be!*

Designing your own world starts with you, becoming all that you are and all that you're meant to be! Becoming doesn't begin and end with you having a goal and achieving it. Becoming isn't about awards, accolades or any type of recognition. Becoming has nothing to do with what others say about you. Becoming isn't about your biography. Becoming has nothing to do with the amount you have in your bank account.

Becoming is a choice — a conscious choice to enjoy the person you're becoming as you embark on your journey to live as the person you were born to be — to live fully and embrace the set of victories and failures that are packaged in your becoming. With time, you will realise that everything that's happened in your life so far needed to happen to enable your becoming. If you hadn't walked the journey you have walked so far, you would not be reading this book. I know there may be parts of your life that you may wish to erase — aspects of your life that you wouldn't dare wish on anyone. We all have experiences in our lives that have left scars — physical and emotional scars — but these challenging experiences help us discover what makes us feel the most alive.

Your experiences have allowed you to develop compassion for others who've gone through the same challenges as you, and that will enable you to make others feel understood in a way they've never felt before. As you become, you will let go of any ill feelings attached to your failures or negative life experiences, and only see the hidden blessings and lessons. These lessons carry the tools to speed up your process of becoming. As you become, make it your priority to clear your heart of anything that makes it feel heavy.

Find peace in knowing that as you become, your growth won't interfere with anyone else's good. Find peace in knowing that your becoming does not need to be approved or accepted by anyone else but yourself — wholeheartedly. Find peace in knowing that what is yours is *yours*. And only you can become in a way that is uniquely yours. You are not competing with others who are also becoming, because there's room for everyone to evolve in their own unique way. In fact, no one can take your 'becoming' away from you. Only you have the power to bring your becoming to a complete stop or to slow it down.

Only you can take the necessary action to move towards your becoming. No one else is qualified for your becoming. You can learn from those who are ten steps ahead of you, or even more, but you are the only one responsible for your progress.

You are currently reading the ideas in this book, which means you have started your journey to become. Something in this book will awaken a knowing that you cannot ignore. You already have a spark in you. Now you just need to apply the principles in this book to see for yourself how mighty your fire is — to see for yourself that you have the power to come alive and light up your world.

Designing your own world is not a one-off project or destination. It's an ongoing process of applying the SMS Formula to bring you one step closer to who you truly are. Designing your own world means living as your best self. Designing your own world basically means to keep on becoming the truest version of yourself, that version of yourself that sets your soul on fire and enables you to light up your world — the world you design.

You are not alone — millions of people want to become, but only a few have access to the ideas in this book. But that's okay. By lighting up your world, you will inspire others around you to light up their world too. Your becoming enables others to see possibilities in themselves through you, and your becoming enables others to become too.

Every chapter in this book has guided you on how to become. Now you just need to become the most authentic version of you! Your becoming begins when you decide to start walking towards your chosen path, with the intention of enjoying, learning and growing from the 'you' that's unfolding right before your eyes.

Opportunity to write

▸ *Who are you becoming?*
▸ *Who do you want to become?*

CHAPTER 12

SEE YOUR BEST, BE YOUR BEST

*Everything you've been through
has led you to this moment.*

Both your good and bad experiences have led you to this moment, even the painful experiences. Those experiences have contributed to your personal growth and have shaped your character. Your past experiences have sharpened your wisdom and have shown you who your true loved ones are. Those experiences have also taught you to be your own cheerleader and to trust your initial hunch or what some may call your 'gut feeling'.

At some point in time, you've been introduced to people who managed to have a glimpse of 'your best', even though you couldn't quite see it yet. While it's easier to see all those who don't see the best in you and be disappointed or frustrated by that, find comfort in knowing that there are people you are not even aware of who have seen the best in you. You've always been special. You've always had all the basics to let 'your best' shine through! But for one reason or another, you've been afraid. You have a fear of failure, of shining too brightly, of falling flat on your face, of losing, of making a mistake, of being laughed at. Or, maybe, you've been afraid to introduce the best you to the world because you might offend, upset or attract unwanted attention in the process.

Someone out there is waiting for you to show up. Sometimes, things in our lives don't work out for a reason. Whatever the reason, just focus on the lesson you learned from that experience. Choose to admire how much stronger you are now. Let go of the memories of all that didn't work out, and hold on tight to the lessons you gained from these experiences. Just because something didn't work out in the past, doesn't mean it won't work out in the future.

Just because you've experienced pain, loss and disappointment before doesn't mean more pain, loss and disappointment await you in the future. You have a brand-new chance waiting for you to realise its worth — use it. Whatever you think is holding you back from getting to where you want to be is imaginary. You've created a mythical monster that found its way into your physical world to scare you — to keep you focused on your past and in denial of the bright future that awaits you, the bright future that was always there for you. Now that you've read the principles in this book, I hope that you'll apply them. And when you do, you will come to realise this:

You have the power to design your own world.
You have the power to take yourself
anywhere you wish to go.

All your wildest dreams can come true if only you find the courage to stand up for what you believe in — if only you choose to show up as the truest version of yourself. Something better awaits you. You deserve to be successful. You deserve to be happy. You deserve to experience extraordinary health. You deserve to have joyful relationships. You deserve to express all of your hidden talents.

All of those things you perceived as obstacles standing between you and your desired results were never as big as you imagined them. In fact, they were tiny. The biggest obstacle was always you. You were delaying, refusing, resisting and sometimes hiding from yourself and your best.

There's no need to be afraid anymore. Just trust yourself. Trust the voice that speaks from your heart. That same voice inspired you to start reading this book and whispers messages of hope to you from time to time. That same voice daydreams of a bright and colourful future and allows your mind to drift into a space where you can literally see the future you want and the world how you wish to design it.

There's enough goodness in you to see through all the dirt that's covering your best. Just choose. Choose to trust. Choose to see. And ask to be reintroduced to the best that lives within you. The best parts of you. Your best has the power to heal and to change lives. And if you don't think so, just try to step into the next best version of yourself and see what happens.

Every life is a little miracle — a blessing that comes to life with its own version of best. See your best now — not the best you were or the best you will be. See the best parts of you at the moment. There's no need to lower your own standard of best to match someone else's definition of best. Your version of best is a perfect match for the person you were born to be. Your version of best is an ideal match to the world you were born to design.

For a long time, I questioned the best parts of me, because I didn't know how to let my best 'live and breathe'. I've come to realise that the next best version of myself was always there — waiting for me to believe in myself from the inside out, not from the outside in. You see, for a long time, I was waiting for the external proof to acknowledge my best — the external validation to believe in my best. I was looking for evidence. When actually I just needed to believe wholeheartedly in my best from the inside first, in order for my best to be evident in the physical world I was living in.

The same concept applies to designing your own world. Designing your own world requires you to be able to see the best in you, and that power which lives in the best parts of you. Designing your own world requires strength and bravery to know where you are now and where you want to be. Designing your own world requires applying the SMS Formula wholeheartedly and patiently watching your desired results unfold.

I appreciate you. It takes strength to start reading a book like this, and it takes courage to implement the principles in this book. And for that reason, I respect you! Many people dream and wish to live in a world that matches their desire, but only a few people make a conscious effort to take the steps required and actually design it.

Not everything in this book will resonate with you the first time you read it. That's okay. Depending on where you are in your life right now, not everything you read will make sense the first time you see it. It might not be easy for you to absorb all the teachings in this book the first time you read it, so I recommend you read this book as many times as you need during this journey.

When you are able to see the best in you now, you will realise that you have everything it takes to design your world. And as you begin to live and learn in the world that you design, other little miracles will be attracted to you too.

When you can finally see the next best version of yourself, then you will be able to see the best in others.

BONUS TOOLS

Our time together and your personal development journey doesn't stop here. Visit the link to download your bonus tools. www.celamade.com/booktools/

Design Your World Newsletter — Stay empowered, educated and inspired with tools and tips to live the life you really want.

Design Your World Guided Visualisation on MP3 Audio — Sit back, relax and start feeding your mind with new possibilities to design your world. (Not for use while driving or operating equipment.)

Design Your World Event — Enjoy some hours of inspiration as Cel helps you to define your next steps and gives you the strategies to achieve it.

DESIGN YOUR WORLD VIRTUAL EVENT FREE TICKET

Cel Amade invites you to attend a Design Your World Virtual Event, as a complimentary participant. To register and get more information on how to claim your ticket, go to www.celamade.com/booktools/ and enter information about your purchase.

This offer is open to anyone who purchases a new edition of *Prepping for the Real World* by Cel Amade from an authorised retailer. Original proof of purchase is required.

This offer is limited to Design Your World Virtual Events only, and your registration for the event is subject to availability of space. A limited number of event complimentary tickets will be made available on a first come, first served basis. This is a limited time offer. All information about these events will be updated regularly at www.celamade.com/booktools/

and are subject to cancellation or to end based on demand. The value of this free admission is approximately £97 as of January 2022, based on comparable events.

Cel Amade reserves the right to remove anyone who is disrupting the event. The distributor of this book is not the sponsor of this offer and is not responsible for its design, operation and fulfilment. Cel Amade is solely responsible for the virtual event's content, operation and fulfilment.

Scan the QR code, and claim your free ticket:

SOME WORDS
OF INSPIRATION

1. Be brave enough to take a stand and ask for what you want.

2. Life will give you what you're brave enough to ask for.

3. The only thing worth changing is your perspective. Let go of the disempowering stories you tell yourself.

4. How you feel in this moment will guide you into the next moment.

5. Your world will change when your perspective about yourself changes.

6. You always had the power. You have everything you need to take yourself there.

7. *You have the power to create and design the world you want to live in, or let your world be designed by others!*

8. *You have the power to choose where you want to be — a place that allows you to stay loyal to who you truly are.*

9. *If you are dissatisfied with where you are now, you owe it to yourself to choose where you want to be.*

10. *Choose a specific result, then take bold, strategic marketing steps in the direction of your desired result.*

11. *Set yourself free of shame, blame, guilt and regret.*

12. *You have no idea how strong you are.*

13. *Give yourself the gift of freedom to design your own world and unleash the person you were born to be.*

14. *You can cheat anyone else but yourself.*

15. *You cannot cheat yourself and design your own world at the same time.*

16. *Regardless of everything you've been through, it's never too late to believe in yourself.*

17. *When you realise who you are, you'll realise how strong you are. You will be brave enough to take a stand for what you believe in, and you will be more than willing to replace any perspective that doesn't empower you to design your own world.*

18. *Designing your own world starts with you!*

19. *The quickest way to get to your desired result is to have fun along the way. The longest way to get to your desired result is to obsess about it — by questioning day in and day out why you haven't arrived at your new destination.*

20. *Designing your own world basically means to become — to become the most authentic version of yourself.*

21. *You are becoming all that you are and all that you're meant to be!*

22. *Designing your own world is not a one-off project. It's an ongoing process of applying the SMS Formula to become one step closer to who you truly are.*

23. *If you want to get to your desired result faster, remember to have fun along the way. You'll be there before you know it!*

24. *It's never too late to believe in who you are and the strength that lives in you — to be brave and to shift any perspective that doesn't serve you well — and to believe that you have the power to design your own world.*

25. *Everything you have been through has led you to this moment.*

26. *See your best qualities now — not the best you were or the best you will be. See the best parts of you at this very moment.*

27. *As you begin to live and learn in the world that you design, other little miracles will be attracted to you too.*

28. *Designing your own world requires you to be able to see your best qualities.*

29. *When you are able to see the best in you now, you will realise that you have everything it takes to design your world.*

30. *See your best, be your best! You are everything the world needs.*

ACKNOWLEDGEMENTS

Thank you to all the superwomen and supermen who inspired me to design my own world.

Mom, you encouraged me to study abroad to give me the best chance to live in my brilliance (even though my departure also meant breaking your heart into a million pieces). Thank you for giving me the chance to be the 'brilliant one' I was born to be.

Marina Albiromi, you came into my life to say the exact words that I needed to hear the most — *You have no idea how strong you are*. I carry your words with me everywhere I go. Thank you for helping me see my strength when I couldn't see it myself!

Lisa Nichols, you helped me shift my life and my world in so many ways. Your encouraging words kept me going through my darkest hours. Listening to you made me feel understood. When I met you for the first time, I watched you live in your light, and that was all I needed to pull myself out of the dark world I had been living in. Thank you for reminding me to let *this little light of mine shine.* Thank you for welcoming me into your world with so much love and for making me feel like I belong. You have taught me so much!

Stefan Ilev, you have seen the best and worst of me. With you, I learned to be brave. To love and to live in my light. Thank you for always encouraging me to shine, especially when I was too afraid to be me. Thank you for your unwavering support and kindness throughout the years. Thank you for showing me what demonstrable love looks like. I love you to the moon and back!

Garri Davis, Ene Obi, Charcee Starks, Jackie Harden, Danita Sajous, Margaret Packer, Esther V. Graham, Dr. Delicia Haynes, Tanya Hall, Marianne Cadet, Nicole Cervantes, Charisa Munroe-Wilborn, Anastarcia Palacious, Dr. Alisha Griffith, Michele Johnson, Tara Woodside, Joy Adams, Sharon D. Carson, Dr. Denise Nicholson, Terri Wade, Dr. Brandy Florence, Leslie Carpenter, Alana Major, Brenda Geary, Darnell Osborne, Karen Hall, Twyla Stubblefield, Dr. Priscilla Jones Akpaita, Dr. Francine Wingster-Riley, Dr. Sue Carter Collins, Veronica Rodgers, Erika Greenwood, Yulonda

Bardney, and Joy Onyesoh, you are my village of consistent love, encouragement and kindness. You inspire me to keep on learning, growing and becoming the next best version of myself. Thank you for helping me spread my wings and trust my soar. I appreciate each and every one of you and value our friendship.

ABOUT THE AUTHOR

Cel Amade has spent the last five years empowering, equipping and educating young adults to recognise their own talents and potential, confidently market their skills and redefine success on their own terms. As a result of her keynotes, courses, coaching and workshops, audiences find themselves more confident about who they're becoming and accelerating their careers faster than most.

Cel is a celebrated speaker in universities, schools, companies and NGOs, and she has helped over 2,500 youth alter the trajectory of their lives — by shifting their cycles of unworthiness and rejection towards believing in their unique strengths and monetising their talents. As an international speaker, she has touched the hearts and minds of young adults, executives, professionals, teachers, teens, students and parents, using her simple yet powerful techniques.

Combined with an inspiring personal history that brought her from Mozambique to England at nineteen, Cel's unique first-hand experiences also strike a chord with global and diverse audiences. She has been featured in TEDx, FE News, Prospects UK, Business Graduate Association, *SAGE Business Cases Publications. The Voice* newspaper, *The AMBITION Podcast* and Enterprise Nation.

Cel has an undergraduate degree in international business and management from Royal Holloway University of London and a postgraduate degree in entrepreneurship from the University of Cambridge. In October 2021, Cel joined the advisory board of the School of Business and Management, Royal Holloway University. She lives, plays and works in Liverpool, England, and she enjoys sharing her Design Your World training programme and encouraging messages with audiences around the world.

Cel conducts one session or up to seven sessions of Design Your World trainings in which she teaches the principles of designing your own world in a powerful life-changing workshop. Her trainings are designed for students, graduates, young adults, founders, educators and others who are interested in taking the lead role in designing their extraordinary lives. To find out more about Cel's workshops, coaching and training, or to enquire about Cel's availability as a speaker or trainer, you can contact her at:

Email: info@celamade.com

www.celamade.com

Stay connected

@Cel Amade

Printed in Great Britain
by Amazon

79684645R00071